OUTLAW SON: THE STORY OF NED KELLY

black dog

PAULA HUNT

For my mum, Gwen

First published in 2009 by  black dog books

This edition reprinted in 2013
by black dog books,
an imprint of Walker Books Australia Pty Ltd
Locked Bag 22, Newtown
NSW 2042 Australia
www.walkerbooks.com.au

Paula Hunt asserts the moral right to be identified
as the author of this Work.

Text © 2009 Paula Hunt

Designed by Blue Boat Design
Printed and bound in China

National Library of Australia
Cataloguing-in-publication data:
Hunt, Paula
Outlaw son: The story of Ned Kelly

Includes Index
For primary school children.
ISBN: 978 1 742030 78 4
Subjects: Kelly, Ned, 1855-1880.
          Bushrangers — Australia — Biography
364.15520994

10 9 8 7 6 5 4

PHOTO CREDITS:
pp 4-5, 17, 23 National Library of Australia;
p 19 National Gallery of Australia.
All other images courtesy of the State Library of Victoria.

black dog would like to thank Dr Brian Wimborne, PhD.,
B.Sc., B. Econ. for his thorough factual check of this book.

CONTENTS

BUSHRANGERS

The Bolters

The first bushranger arrived in Australia with the First Fleet in 1788. John "Black" Caesar, a convict transported for the theft of £12, could not live on the meagre food rations he was given, so he escaped, stealing food to stay alive.

These first bushrangers were known as The Bolters. They were mostly convicts transported to Australia as punishment for crimes committed in Britain. Some of these sad men went bush to escape the inhuman conditions of the penal settlements, thieving to survive. Some, however, were just depraved criminals.

This era of bushranging included the gentleman bushrangers, Matthew Brady and Martin Cash, the murderous Michael Howe and the cannibal Alexander Pearce.

4

Police photograph of Ned Kelly

Local Outlaws

By the mid 1850s, **transportation** to the eastern **colonies** had stopped, and Australia was in the midst of a gold rush.

The new bushranger was a local lad, born and bred in Australia. He was an excellent horseman and knew the bush like the back of his hand. **Cattle duffing**, **horse planting** and horse stealing were commonplace. Many young men hardly saw it as a crime at all.

Frank "Darkie" Gardiner (who masterminded the biggest hold-up in bushranging history), Bold Ben Hall, and the professional bushranger Captain Thunderbolt, are just a few of the hundreds of bushrangers from this era.

Bushrangers holding up coach passengers—Patrick William Marony

The Last Stand

By the early 1870s, a more extensive police force, assisted by an ever-improving rail and telegraph system, had seen the Australian bushranger all but eliminated.

But there was to be one last era, one last stand. And it would be dominated by the most famous bushranger of all time—Ned Kelly.

"I am called the blackest and coldest blooded murderer ever on record."

Ned Kelly—*The Jerilderie Letter*

"Who knows the Kelly Country? How far does it extend?

Is it a dream or legend that has not start nor end?

The outlaws ride no longer but like the afterglow

Their spirits haunt the ranges they rode long years ago."[★]

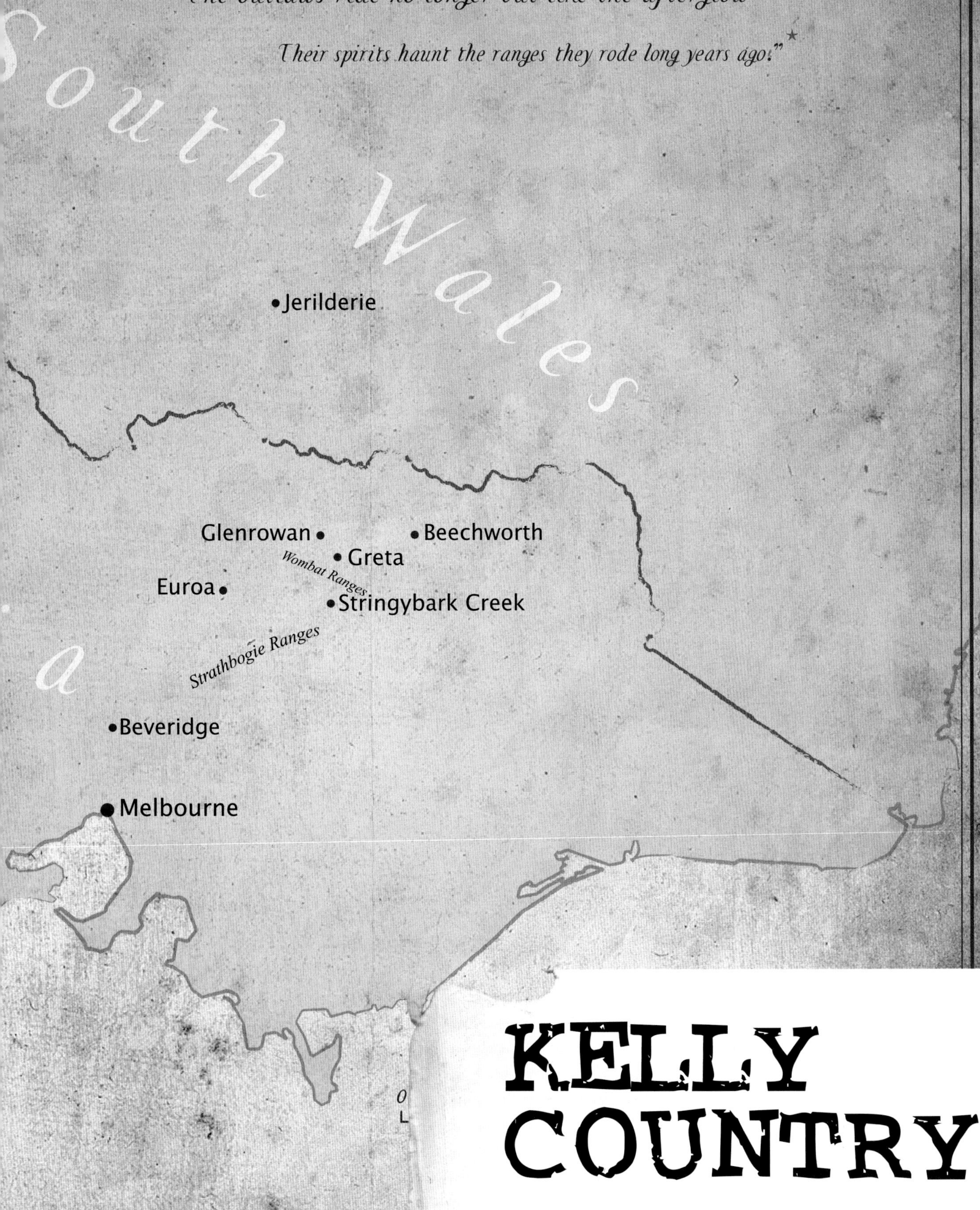

South Wales

a

● Jerilderie

Glenrowan ●　　　● Beechworth

● Greta

Wombat Ranges

Euroa ●

● Stringybark Creek

Strathbogie Ranges

● Beveridge

● Melbourne

KELLY COUNTRY

Gold

Australia in the 1850s wasn't a country but a collection of British **colonies**. The discovery of gold saw a population explosion in the colony of Victoria—but it also brought dispute. Led by Irishman Peter Lalor, the **diggers** in Ballarat built a stockade and took up arms against the government troops, in protest against unfair licence fees. The Eureka Stockade became a symbol of rebellion against corrupt authority. Ned Kelly was born not long after the Eureka Stockade.

The Colony of Victoria

By the 1870s, when Ned was a young man, railways had begun to spread out from Melbourne and through the Victorian countryside. Melbourne had become a bustling city where anyone could enjoy a day at the horse races or the football.

8

1788
First Fleet arrives in Botany Bay with John "Black" Caesar on board.

1788
Colony of New South Wales founded.

1820
Red Kelly born.

1832
Ellen Quinn born.

THE AUSTRALIAN
PICTORIAL WEEKLY
AN ILLUSTRATED NEWSPAPER.

No. 7.   MELBOURNE, SATURDAY, JULY 24, 1880.   PRICE 3D.
Per Year, 12s.

SKETCH AT THE FOOTBALL MATCH.
CARLTON v. GEELONG.
GEORGE COULTHARD RUNNING WITH THE BALL.

"If a poor man happened to leave his horse or bit of a poddy calf outside his paddock they would be impounded."

Ned Kelly—*The Jerilderie Letter*

Squatter v Selector

But in the country, where Ned grew up, the **squatters** still controlled large sections of the best land. The **squattocracy**, as they were known, were very powerful. The government, in an effort to break the squatters' stranglehold, allowed free settlers to acquire, or select, a small piece of land to work.

The squatters disliked the **selectors**; **dummying** (using another person to purchase land for you to avoid the laws limiting the amount of land one person could own) and **peacocking** ("picking the eyes" out of a run by selecting the best bits of land) were commonplace. If a selector's cattle wandered onto the squatter's land, the squatter would charge a fee for the return of the cattle.

Many of the squatters were of English descent, while the selectors were often poor Irish. For some the battle between squatters and selectors was more than just a dispute between neighbours— it was a clash between rich and poor, between English and Irish.

1837

Governor Bourke declares Port Phillip a settlement.

1841

Red Kelly transported to Australia.

1841

Ellen Quinn comes to Australia with her family.

GROWING UP KELLY

John "Red" Kelly was a freed Irish convict when he met and married 18 year old Ellen Quinn. The couple had eight children over their sixteen-year marriage, five girls and three boys. Their oldest boy was christened Edward—Ned for short.

Red had dreams of supporting his family as a farmer, so he bought some land near Beveridge in Victoria. But Red was never able to make the farm pay, and he had to sell up.

Ned's extended family was always in trouble with the law. His cousins and uncles were arrested for everything from cattle stealing to assaulting police. When Ned was ten years old his father spent time in jail. And Ned himself was just 14 when he was arrested for assault, although the charges were later dismissed.

Ned went to school in Avenel untill he was 11, passing reading and writing at fourth class level. But when Red died Ellen took up a **selection**, moving the family to Eleven Mile Creek, near Greta in Victoria. It was a tough existence.

The township of Greta

Young Ned became a local hero when he jumped into a river and saved a small boy, Dick Shelton, from drowning. The Shelton family gave Ned a green sash to commend his bravery.

1845

Red Kelly is given a Ticket-of-Leave.

1848

Red Kelly is a free man.

1850 NOV

Red and Ellen marry.

1851

Mary Kelly born. Dies in infancy.

> "Bail Up!"—This is what Harry and Ned would yell at travellers they were robbing. It meant "stop and hand over your valuables".

```
                        John "Red" Kelly
                   Ellen Kelly (nee Quinn)
```

Mary Kelly 1851 (died in infancy)	Anne Kelly 1853	Edward (Ned) Kelly 1855 Exact date unknown	Margaret (Maggie) Kelly 1857	James (Jim) Kelly 1858	Dan Kelly 1861	Catherine (Kate) Kelly 1863	Grace Kelly 1865

Harry Power

Harry Power was a career bushranger who was active during all three eras of bushranging. When Ned was still a teenager he became Harry's "apprentice", bailing up people in the Strathbogie Ranges. But after a few months Ned got tired of riding with Power and he went home to his mother and siblings. The police arrested Ned for **robbery under arms**, but after some time and several court appearances, Ned was released.

11

1851

Victoria becomes a separate colony.

1851

Gold discovered. Gold rush begins.

1853

End of transportation of convicts from England to east coast colonies.

FIGHTING & STEALING

Ned's first conviction, and serious stint in jail, was not for horse stealing or robbery under arms. When he was 15 he got involved in a fight between two **hawkers**. He was charged with violent assault, and when his family could not pay the fine he spent nearly five months in jail.

> "Every one looks on me like a black snake."
>
> Ned met Sergeant Babington when he had been charged with robbery under arms. Ned later wrote to him asking for help, as he felt he had become an outcast.

> "I don't think I would use a revolver to shoot a man like him...while I had a pairs of arms and bunch of fives on the end of them that never failed to peg out anything they came into contact with..."
>
> Ned later talks about his fighting abilities in *The Jerilderie Letter.*

1853 NOV

Anne Kelly born.

1854 DEC

Eureka rebellion.

1855

Ned Kelly born. Exact date not known.

1856

Victorian stonemasons are the first in the world to win the right to an eight hour working day.

Three Years Hard Labour

Ned served his sentence and had only been released for a short time when he was charged with receiving a stolen horse. He claimed that he didn't know the horse had been stolen but was convicted of the crime and sentenced to three years hard labour in prison.

The Kelly family thought they were always being persecuted by the authorities. That assumption appeared justified when the man who was charged with actually stealing the horse received only half Ned's sentence.

When Ned got out of jail he was a grown man. For several years he kept out of trouble, working as a **bullocky**, felling trees and breaking horses, but the police continued to hound him. Eventually he became involved in cattle duffing and horse stealing with a gang of friends and family. The gang included, among others, Ned's new stepfather George King and two friends, Joe Byrne and Aaron Sherritt.

The Victorian Mounted Police Force

"I began to think they wanted me to give them something to talk about. Therefore I started wholesale and retail horse and cattle dealing"

Ned Kelly in *The Jerilderie Letter*

1857

Margaret (Maggie) Kelly born.

1857

Joe Byrne born.

1858

Melbourne Grammar School play Scotch College in what is considered the first game of "Aussie Rules".

THE FITZPATRICK AFFAIR

On the 15 April 1878, Constable Alexander Fitzpatrick went to the Kelly home at Eleven Mile Creek to arrest Ned's younger brother, Dan, on a charge of horse stealing. Fitzpatrick returned without Dan, but with a bandaged wrist and a dint in his helmet. He claimed Dan Kelly had resisted arrest, and Ned Kelly had shot him.

But Constable Fitzpatrick was not a man people trusted (sometime later he was discharged from the police, accused of dishonesty and drunkenness).

Ned said he wasn't even at the house when Fitzpatrick came to arrest his brother. And numerous witnesses say the problem started when Fitzpatrick, who knew the Kellys, tried to kiss Ned's younger sister, Kate.

In the end Ellen Kelly, neighbour William "Brickey" Williamson, and Ellen's son-in-law, Bill Skilling, were charged with attempted murder. Orders for the arrest of Dan and Ned were issued.

After the Fitzpatrick incident, Ned and Dan fled into the bush. Hoping to make money for their mother's defence, they panned for gold and grew crops for making whiskey. But it all came to nothing.

14

1858

James (Jim) Kelly born.

1860

Burke and Wills set off from Melbourne on expedition to travel to the Gulf of Carpentaria.

1860

Steve Hart born.

1861

Dan Kelly born.

Mrs Kelly and family outside the homestead

Ellen had a new baby, only two days old, when Fitzpatrick had come knocking, but that didn't sway the judge, Redmond Barry. Ellen was sentenced to three years hard labour and the two men to six years each. Ned later claimed Bill Skilling wasn't even at Eleven Mile Creek at the time of the incident, and that Fitzpatrick had mistaken Joe Byrne for Skilling.

"(Fitzpatrick) pulled out his revolver and said he would blow her brains out if she interfered in the arrest. Mrs Kelly said that if Ned was here he would ram the revolver down his throat."

Ned Kelly gives his account of what happened at Eleven Mile Creek in *The Cameron Letter.*

15

1861

Archer wins the first Melbourne Cup.

1862

Frank "Darkie" Gardiner commits Eugowra robbery. Biggest robbery in bushranging history.

1863

State funeral held for Burke and Wills.

THE KELLY GANG

Ned was furious with the harsh sentence given to his mother, and his hatred for the authorities grew. He and Dan remained in hiding and a reward of £100 was offered for their capture. They were soon joined by Steve Hart and Joe Byrne. These four young men became the Kelly Gang.

Dan Kelly

Like his big brother Ned, Dan was an excellent horseman and in trouble with the law from a young age. Dan was a member of the Greta Mob. The Greta Mob had a distinctive dress style—long hair, hat on an angle, colourful sash around the waist and hat stra[p] under the nose.

The Kelly Gang

16

1863

Catherine (Kate) Kelly born.

1865 MAY

Red sentenced to six months for unlawful possession of a hide.

1865 AUG

Grace Kelly born.

1866

Ned saves Dick Shelton from drowning.

Steve Hart

One of Dan's best mates was Steve Hart. Steve grew up on his father's farm on the outskirts of Wangaratta. Steve was jockey-sized, and his superb riding skills were known around the district. Steve had just been released from serving eleven months of a one-year sentence at Beechworth Gaol when Ned asked him to join the Kelly Gang. He was only eighteen years old but he didn't hesitate.

> **"Here's to a short life and a merry one."**
>
> Reportedly said by Steve Hart when Ned Kelly asked him to join his gang.

Dan Kelly, Steve Hart, Ned Kelly, Joe Byrne, Kate Kelly—Patrick William Marony

Joe Byrne

Joe Byrne was good mates with Ned. He was well educated, a crack shot and women thought him dashing. He grew up on the goldfields, spoke Cantonese and was an opium addict. He and his friend Aaron Sherrit had joined Ned and George King in their cattle duffing and horse stealing operation. So when Ned and Dan went bush, Joe quickly joined them.

> **"...for a bushman, rather clever with his pen."**
>
> Police Superintendent Hare about Joe Byrne. Ned Kelly dictated *The Cameron Letter* and *The Jerilderie Letter* to Joe.

1866

Registration of Brands Act made law. Horse-stealing dramatically declines.

1866 DEC

Red dies. Ellen moves the family to Eleven Mile Creek.

1869

Ned becomes Harry Power's apprentice

STRINGYBARK CREEK

The Kelly Gang had been hiding out in the Wombat Ranges for six months when four policemen—McIntyre, Scanlon, Kennedy and Lonigan—rode out from Mansfield in search of them. On their first night the **troopers** made camp at Stringybark Creek. They didn't know it, but they were less than two kilometres from the Kelly Gang.

The next day, Ned and the boys attacked the camp, and in the commotion Lonigan was shot dead by Ned. McIntyre surrendered. Kennedy and Scanlon were away from the camp but were due back soon. As they waited, the gang ate the food McIntyre had made for the troopers.

When Kennedy and Scanlon returned, McIntyre tried to warn them, but the troopers thought McIntyre was joking. They changed their minds, though, when Ned jumped up from behind a log and yelled, "Bail up! Hold your hands up!" In the chaos that followed both Scanlon and Kennedy were shot dead. Tragically, Kennedy was shot by Ned after he had tried to surrender, but Ned had mistakenly thought the trooper was turning to shoot him. McIntyre escaped into the bush, spending the night in a wombat hole before walking back to Mansfield.

The gang had killed three policemen and left nine children fatherless. The reward was increased to £500 for each member of the Kelly Gang—a fortune in those days. And anyone helping the Kelly gang (**sympathisers**) could get fifteen years in jail.

1869 OCT

Ned is acquitted of assault and robbery charges relating to an incident with Chinese hawker Ah Fook.

1870

Harry Power captured.

1870

Bushranger Fred Ward, "Captain Thunderbolt", is shot dead by police.

1870

Ned held for seven weeks on charge of robbery under arms. Case dropped.

> "I would have scattered their blood and brains like rain, I would manure the Eleven Mile with their bloated carcasses, and yet remember there is not one drop of murderous blood in my veins."

Ned Kelly, *The Jerilderie Letter*. Ned was angry about the police raiding the houses of his friends.

Death of Sergeant Kennedy at Stringybark Creek—Sidney Nolan, National Gallery of Australia

> "...as he slewed around to surrender I did not know he had dropped his revolver."

Ned Kelly's account of the Kennedy shooting in *The Jerilderie Letter*.

19

1870 MAY
Ned writes a letter to Sergeant Babington to ask for assistance.

1870 JUL
Ned sentenced to six months for assault and obscene language.

1870 OCT
Ellen Kelly gives birth to a baby (Ellen). The father is Bill Frost.

THE EUROA BANK ROBBERY

The police hunt for the Kelly gang was plagued by bungling; still, Ned knew he needed the support of the gang's families and friends. That loyalty would be more easily secured if they had money. He concocted a brilliant plan to rob the National Bank in Euroa.

The day before they planned to rob the bank, Ned and the boys held up a homestead at Faithfull's Creek, locking all the workers in the storehouse. The homestead would now be their base.

The next day they cut the telegraph wires, donned disguises and headed into town. Joe was left at the station to look after the hostages. Late that afternoon Ned, Dan and Steve forced their way into the bank and stole about £2000 in cash and gold. They then rounded up the bank employees and bank manager's family and took them on a cart back to the station at Faithfull's Creek.

At the station, Ned and the boys had something to eat and entertained their captives, before riding off with their loot.

1871

Dan Kelly charged with illegally using a horse. Discharged.

1871 MAR

Ned gets out of jail.

1871 AUG

Ned sentenced to three years for receiving a stolen horse.

1872

Ellen Kelly's baby (Ellen) to Bill Frost dies.

The Kelly gang at Euroa

The Cameron Letter

Ned Kelly thought of himself as an honest man, forced into a life of crime by crooked police who victimised him. Ned dictated a letter to Joe Byrne trying to explain his actions, but he also threatened police if they continued to hound him and his family.

Joe made two copies of the letter. One was sent to a politician called Donald Cameron, the second to one of the policemen tracking the Kelly Gang. That letter is now known as *The Cameron Letter*.

"This sort of cruelty and disgraceful conduct to my brothers and sisters who had no protection, coupled with the conviction of my Mother and those innocent men certainly made my blood boil as I don't think there is a man born could have the patience to suffer what I did."

Ned Kelly in *The Cameron Letter*

1872

Anne Gunn (nee Kelly) dies giving birth.

1873

Jim Kelly sentenced to five years for cattle stealing.

1873 DEC

Anna Gunn (Anne Gunn's daughter) dies.

JERILDERIE

Only a few months after the robbery at Euroa the gang were at it again, at Jerilderie in New South Wales. This time the robbery took three days and was as daring, and at times as **farcical** a robbery as ever took place.

Cheekily, Ned and the boys took over the police station as their base, locking the two local troopers in their own jail with a drunk. The next day, a Sunday, they dressed as policemen and patrolled the town.

On the Monday morning the gang had their horses re-shod before taking over a hotel, holding hostage the people they gathered in the parlour. Ned and Joe headed next door to the bank. When it became apparent they would need the bank manager to open the main safe, Joe and Ned, with the help

The Kelly's visit to the police station, Jerilderie

of the bank accountant, Edwin Living, retrieved the bank manager from his bath. Unfortunately for Ned and the boys, when they eventually rode out of town they only had a bit over £2000 from the robbery. They had been hoping for a lot more.

The reward for the gang was raised to £8000, an extraordinary amount for the time.

> "The kindest man I ever met."
>
> Mrs Divine, the policeman's wife at Jerilderie, on Ned Kelly.

1873

Maggie Kelly marries Bill Skilling and they have a baby (Ellen).

1874 FEB

Ellen Kelly marries American George King and they have a baby (Ellen).

1874 FEB

Ned released from Pentridge Prison (Melbourne).

1875

Ellen gives birth to a son, John.

The Jerilderie Letter

At Jerilderie, Ned dictated another long letter to Joe telling his side of the story. It was similar to *The Cameron Letter*, but angrier. Ned wanted the letter to be printed so everyone could read it, but the town's newspaper editor, Gill, had escaped. Ned left the letter with Living, who promised to give it to Gill. Living didn't keep his promise.

> "A little bit of my life."
>
> Kelly's words as he handed *The Jerilderie Letter* to Living.

EDWARD (NED) KELLY

This photo was taken in Benalla, September, 1877, the day Ned had the fight with the four policemen outside the Benalla Court House.

This photo was taken the day prior to his being hanged. He asked for a nice photo for his mother to keep, and went to great pains to attend to his appearance.

V. R.

£8000 REWARD
ROBBERY and MURDER.

WHEREAS EDWARD KELLY, DANIEL KELLY, STEPHEN HART and JOSEPH BYRNE have been declared OUTLAWS in the Colony of Victoria, and whereas warrants have been issued charging the aforesaid men with the WILFUL MURDER of MICHAEL SCANLON, Police Constable of the Colony of VICTORIA, and whereas the above-named offenders are STILL at LARGE, and have recently committed divers felonies in the Colony of NEW SOUTH WALES; Now, therefore, I, SIR HERCULES GEORGE ROBERT ROBINSON, the GOVERNOR, do, by this, my proclamation issued with the advice of the Executive Council, hereby notify that a REWARD of £4,000 will be paid, three-fourths by the Government of NEW SOUTH WALES, and one fourth by certain Banks trading in the Colony, for the apprehension of the above-named Four Offenders, or a reward of £1000 for the apprehension of any one of them; and that, in ADDITION to the above reward, a similar REWARD of £4000 has been offered by the Government of VICTORIA, and I further notify that the said REWARD will be equitably apportioned between any persons giving information which shall lead to the apprehension of the offenders and any members of the police force or other persons who may actually effect such apprehension or assist thereat.

(Signed) HENRY PARKES,
Colonial Secretary, New South Wales.

(Signed) BRYAN O'LOGHLEN,
Attorney General, Victoria.

> "I am a widows son outlawed and my orders must be obeyed."
>
> Ned signs off *The Jerilderie Letter*

23

1876 OCT.

Dan Kelly charged with stealing a saddle. Discharged.

1877

Jim Kelly sentenced to ten years for horse stealing.

1877 MAR

Dan Kelly charged again with stealing a saddle. Discharged.

FRIENDS & ENEMIES

Armour

The gang laid low for nearly 16 months. During that time Ned had the gang's famous armour made from plough mould-boards (the curved metal plates of a plough that push the earth aside). Ned's armour, which weighed over 40 kilograms, consisted of a helmet, a breast plate, a back plate, shoulder guards and a flap at the front to protect his groin.

> "...big, ugly fat-necked wombat headed big bellied magpie legged narrow hipped splaw footed sons of Irish Bailiffs or English landlords which is better known as Officers of Justice or Victoria Police."
>
> Ned Kelly in *The Jerilderie Letter*

1877 JUL — Steve Hart sentenced to twelve months for unlawfully using a horse.

1877 SEP — Ned is fined for being drunk and resisting arrest. Fitzpatrick and Lonigan involved.

1877 OCT — Dan Kelly sentenced to three months for wilful damage.

1878 APR — Ellen gives birth to a daughter, Alice

Aaron Sherritt

Aaron was a close friend of Joe Byrne and knew the Kellys well. He had flirted with the young Kate Kelly, been part of Ned's cattle duffing and horse stealing operation, and was engaged at one time to Joe's sister. When Aaron took up his own selection, Ned and Joe helped him fence the property.

Ned and the boys relied on their friends, the sympathisers, to stay one step ahead of the police. Those friends risked hefty sentences for helping the gang. Aaron Sherritt played the risky role of double agent. He became a paid informant for the police, providing them with information on the gang, while at the same time maintaining his friendship with Joe Byrne. But Joe's mother was suspicious of Aaron, and convinced Ned and Joe that their friend could no longer be trusted.

It was a Saturday night in June, and Aaron was at home near Beechworth with his wife, when there was a knock at the door. When Aaron opened the door, Joe Byrne, his old mate, shot him dead. The four policemen who were in the house to protect Aaron stayed under the bed until the next morning.

The murder of Aaron Sherritt

> "Dear Aaron it is best for you to join us Aaron a short life and a jolly one."
>
> Joe Byrne in a letter to Sherritt a year before he shot him.

1878 APR

Fitzpatrick visits Kelly house to arrest Dan and is injured.

1878 JUN

Steve Hart released from jail.

1878 OCT

Ellen Kelly sentenced to three years for attempted murder.

1878 OCT

Stringybark Creek killings.

GLENROWAN- THE LAST STAND

Ned knew that shooting Aaron would bring a trainload of police to Beechworth, so he had a section of the track pulled up at Glenrowan to derail the train before it could reach its destination. The Gang then holed up at the Glenrowan Inn and waited. They held over 60 people hostage at the inn with them. As they waited the group drank and danced.

Luckily for the police and journalists on the train, Ned allowed the local schoolteacher, Thomas Curnow, to leave the hotel with his family. Curnow, using a candle and a red scarf to stop the train, warned the police of the danger.

Thanks to Curnow the police arrived safely. They surrounded the hotel and began shooting wildly, disregarding the innocent men, women and children inside. Ned, protected by his armour, had come outside to fight back. He was shot several times in his arm and foot, but continued to fight. In the hotel, Joe was shot in the thigh and bled to death. Ned tried to get back to the hotel to save Dan and Steve, but he was shot in the leg and captured.

Once the hostages had escaped from the hotel, it was set on fire. But Dan and Steve had already committed suicide. Their bodies were burned beyond recognition.

The police had been incompetent in their efforts to capture the Kelly Gang. The shoot-out at the Glenrowan Hotel was no exception. Several people, including a young boy, were fatally wounded by the police.

Nevertheless, Dan, Steve and Joe were dead. Ned was in custody. The Kelly Gang was no more.

1878 NOV

The Kelly Gang declared outlaws. Reward £500.

1878 DEC

Kelly Gang robs bank at Euroa.

1879 JAN

Suspected accomplices of the Kellys arrested.

Wangaratta police at the capture of Ned Kelly

"The Queen must surely be proud of such heroic men as the Police...as it takes eight or eleven of the biggest mud crushers in Melbourne to take one poor little half starved larrakin to a watch house."

Ned Kelly in *The Jerilderie Letter*

The capture of Ned Kelly

When Joe Byrne's body was searched they found a prayer book and a bag of poison. He was wearing trooper Scanlon's rings.

1879 FEB

Kelly Gang robs bank at Jerilderie.

1879

Reward increased to £8000.

1879 DEC

Aaron Sherritt is married.

1880

Economic boom hits.

Ned was charged with murder. After a trial, he was found guilty, and Judge Redmond Barry sentenced him to be hanged.

It had been Barry's over-zealous sentencing of Ellen Kelly that had, in part, triggered the events that followed. When he was sentenced, Ned told Judge Barry, "I will see you there—where I go". Sure enough, some weeks later, the judge was dead.

Ellen Kelly, still in prison, was allowed to see her eldest son before he died.

There was a lot of public support for Ned. He had always been courteous to women and kind to children. For many, he was a victim of police corruption and a system that favoured the rich. A petition to save his life gathered over 30 000 signatures in only a few days, but it did not save his life.

Ned Kelly was hanged on 11 November, 1880.

"Such is life."

Purported last words of Ned Kelly as he went to the gallows.

1880

Jim Kelly released from prison.

1880 JUN

Joe Byrne shoots Aaron Sherritt.

1880 JUN

Glenrowan shoot-out. Dan, Steve and Joe killed.

1880 OCT

Ned sentenced to death for murder.

After Ned

The police had some responsibility in the Kelly affair. The way local police had treated the Kelly family had fuelled Ned's rage, and later they had completely bungled all attempts to capture the gang. There was a scathing Royal Commission into the police the following year.

The Ned Kelly legend lived on and grew, inextricably a part of Australian history. After Ned's death, young men would call out "**Game as Ned**" to encourage their mates to be brave. And regardless of how Ned Kelly is viewed—as a criminal or hero of the downtrodden—his relentless fighting spirit cannot be questioned.

Ned Kelly being led to the scaffold

"Now, you daring young fellows take warning by me,
Beware of bushranging, and bad company,
For like many other you may feel the dart
Which pierced the two Kellys, Joe Byrne, and Steve Hart."*

1880 NOV
100 000 people watch Grand Flaneur win the Melbourne Cup.

1880 11 NOV
Ned hanged.

1880 23 NOV
Judge Redmond Barry dies.

1881
Royal Commission into the police.

GLOSSARY

bullocky
man driving a bullock-dray, which was a large cart pulled by bullocks.

cattle duffing
stealing cattle then changing the brand so the cattle could not be traced.

colony
a country (or part of a country) that is settled and controlled by another country.

digger
a gold prospector.

dummying
using another person to purchase land for you to avoid the laws limiting the amount of land one person could own.

farcical
ludicrous, absurd, humorous.

game
the "game" was bushranging.

game, to be
to have pluck, courage and bravery.

hawker
hawkers travelled from place to place selling goods that they carried with them.

horse planting
stealing a horse and then collecting the reward for finding it.

peacocking
"picking the eyes" out of a run by selecting only the prime areas of land, such as land with waterholes.

robbery under arms
using a weapon or firearm in a robbery.

selection
a section of land chosen by a free settler (a "selector").

squatter
someone who settled on large tracts of land without government permission and later gained a lease, sometimes becoming a rich and influential landowner.

squattocracy
the well-established and rich squatters who regarded themselves as aristocrats.

sympathisers
anyone helping the Kelly Gang. They could be jailed for up to 15 years.

Ticket-of-Leave
given to convicts not believed to be of further threat. It allowed them to work and move about in an allocated area until they had completed their sentence.

trooper
police on horseback.

transportation
because the prisons in England were overflowing, convicted criminals were sent to Australia's penal settlements to serve their time.

REFERENCES

Selected Bibilography

Boxall, George, *An Illustrated History of Australian Bushrangers*, Penguin 1988 (original text published in London in 1899 as *Story of the Australian Bushrangers*).

Fearn-Wannan, W., *Australian Folklore: A dictionary of Lore, Legends and Popular Allusions*, Lansdowne, 1970. ★ Extract from *Kelly Country* on page 7 and *Ye Sons of Australia* on page 29 sourced from this text.

Jones, Ian, *Ned Kelly: A Short Life*, Lothian, 1995

Nixon, Allan, *Stand and Deliver! 100 Australian Bushrangers 1789-1901*, Lothian, 1991

Wilkinson, Carole, *Black Snake*, black dog books, 2002

Internet Resources

Australian Dictionary of Biography – Online Edition
www.adb.online.anu.edu.au/adblonline.htm

The Jerilderie Letter can be viewed online at the State Library of Victoria's website
http://www.slv.vic.gov.au/collections/treasures/jerilderieletter/jerilderie01.html

Acknowledgements

Thank you to Andrew Kelly and Maryann Ballantyne for putting me on the trail of Ned.

Thanks also to Melissa and everyone else at black dog for all their hard work.

Thanks to Sue Phelan and David Studham for their help.

INDEX